Know Your Cat's
Purr Points

For my darling mother (1914-2000),
who knew all the purr points

Library of Congress Cataloging-in-Publication Data
Woodhouse, Margaret.
Know your cat's purr points : the art of cat massage / Margaret Woodhouse.
     p. cm.
ISBN: 0-7407-2215-8
    1. Cats—Diseases—Alternative treatment. 2. Massage for animals. I. Title.
SF985.W66 2002
636.8'0895822—dc21   2001053277

First published by Magari Publishing in New Zealand, 2000

Know Your Cat's
Purr Points

The Art of Cat Massage

Margaret Woodhouse

**Andrews McMeel
Publishing**

Kansas City

Contents

▲▲▲▲▲▲▲

The Pleasuring of Cats

▲▲▲▲▲▲▲

The giving of pleasure to a cat is an ancient practice. Through the aeons cats have held sway over humans, bewitching them into conducting indulgent acts of pleasuring. Even Stone Age cat gladly accepted attention from its *Homo sapiens* cave-mate.

The practice reached its zenith in ancient Egypt. But only recently have experts appreciated the extent to which the Egyptians considered the pleasuring of a cat such a practical art. While the receipt of pleasure was a most sensual experience for the subject, the practitioner approached his task in a manner that was both functional and technical.

The art of pleasuring cats has never been lost completely. Now, appropriately in this revivalist age, exciting new finds in Egypt have enabled pleasurecatologists to reconstruct the original Egyptian teachings. These Purr Points are reproduced here, ensuring that full prides of happy cats will endure through the millennia.

Indulgent Locations

It is of extreme importance for the Purr-Point practitioner to know exactly in which location to position the subject when wishing to undertake the pleasuring of a cat.

We recommend the following as excellent choices:

> Armchairs (the ancient Egyptians used thrones)
> Beds (comforters and covers that show claw marks are preferred)
> Kitchen tables
> Wide human laps
> Outdoor sunny locations (flower beds prove
> highly acceptable to subjects)

Remember, positioning is everything!

The Pleasuring of the Front

▲▲▲▲▲▲▲

Ancient writings indicate exactly where the critical Purr Points are on a cat. The practitioner must commit these to memory. Nothing distracts the subject more than an ill-directed application. (It can also be rather dangerous for the practitioner.)

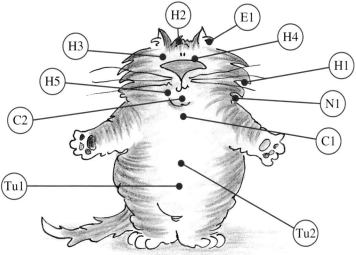

H1	The Interwhisker Side Step	C1	Chin Lifter
H2	The Rumbler	C2	Ticklers
H3	Knuckle Dusters	N1	The Flamenco Guitar
H4	La Petite	Tu1	The Full Fluff
H5	The Transwhisker Cross Step	Tu2	The Plunge
E1	Feather Dusters		

The Pleasuring of the Back

▲▲▲▲▲▲

Note that there are fewer critical Purr Points for the back. This reduced sensitivity would appear to result from a failure on the part of most subjects to shoulder responsibility.

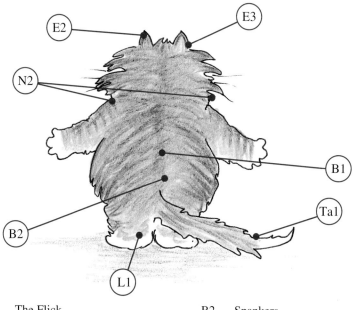

E2	The Flick	B2	Spankers
E3	Tipping	Ta1	The Bell Pull
N2	Double Doses	L1	The Tree Fern
B1	Dancing the Limbo		

The Purr Register

▲▲▲▲▲▲

It is not easy to assess the level of pleasure derived by a cat.

For this reason we have developed two pleasure indicators—a modern but excellent addition to the art of pleasuring the cat.

Each Purr Point is given a rating on both indicators. The practitioner needs to assess both auditory and visual responses. Thus a rating of only II on the Purrometer may be offset by a pose of exquisite response on the Purr Register, lifting the overall score to 4.

Purrs are gauged by the Purrometer—from I to V. Thus:

I–II "The Moped"
Felt only by a few practitioners, mainly those wearing light apparel.

III "The Harley Davidson"
Felt by nearly all practitioners. Negligible movement by subject.

IV "The Corvette"
Felt by all practitioners. Some shift in subject's original position occurs. Fur slightly displaced.

V "The Dump Truck"
Felt, even through cushions. Damage through clawing possible. Few if any practitioners left sitting.

The second of the two pleasure indicators is the Purr Register. As some subjects never purr very much, this highly accurate pleasure assessor allocates a purr level to the nonpurrer, judged on looks alone.

1–2 Pleasant repose

3 Mild enjoyment

4 Pleased to be disturbed

5 Exquisite response

Cautions

Before embarking on any full-scale pleasuring, the practitioner should first
be aware of the following Claw Points:

Never surprise the subject with a
vigorous application. (But see
Spankers on page 54.)

Never attempt an antifurwise
application unless otherwise
instructed.

Should the practitioner accidentally touch a Claw Point, *never* withdraw the hand quickly.

And remember, enough is almost invariably enough!

Head Points

▲▲▲▲▲▲▲

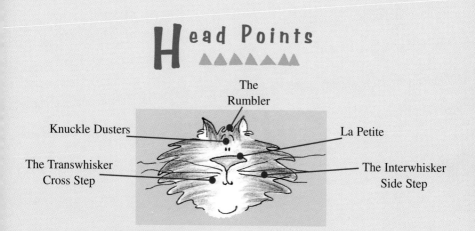

The
Rumbler

Knuckle Dusters

La Petite

The Transwhisker
Cross Step

The Interwhisker
Side Step

When the human polishes the whiskers of a cat
into glittering threads, that is when the lord will
be content to be bound to the slave.

The Interwhisker Side Step

Technique

1.

Subject should have head fully accessible.

2.

This is a single-full-finger action. Hold hand thus. The aim is to achieve a world-is-at-peace-and-the-dog-is-outside feeling.

3.

Rub finger rhythmically up and down cheek and between whiskers until purring is experienced. Moving the finger in a circular motion can also prove effective.

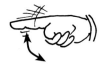

 **Response**

Purrometer reading: V

Rating on the Purr Register: 4

(Important: Do not prolong the ecstasy unduly. Extended application
  provokes needling on the part of the subject. This can be the cause
  of great discomfort to the practitioner.)

H2　The Rumbler

Technique

1.

Many locations will suffice for the Rumbler. However, it is difficult to execute if subject is in full flight.

2.

Practitioner's hand is held thus.

3.

Practitioner moves hand in a furwise direction. Be careful to lift hand for each application. (If considering counterapplication, see Cautions, page 12.)

 # Response

Purrometer reading: III

Rating on the Purr Register: 4

This is unquestionably the classic pleasure. Many applications may be
    conferred every day, and by copious practitioners.

H3   Knuckle Dusters

 Technique

1.

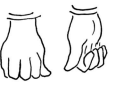

Subject's head must be upright and alert. While it is acceptable to apply Knuckle Dusters while the subject is standing, the sitting position gives maximum stability.

2.

Practitioner's hand should be half-fisted.

3.

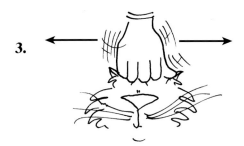

Hold half-fist tautly and, using maximum control, vibrate back and forth with vigor.

Response

Purrometer reading: IV

Rating on the Purr Register: 5

Knuckle Dusters catches the subject in an irresistible insist-desist cycle.

(H4) La Petite

▲▲▲▲▲▲▲

Technique

1.

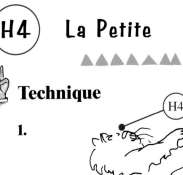

H4

Subject can repose at leisure provided that nose is accessible. Note: This Purr Point is for the bridge of subject's nose, not the moist health indicator at the end.*

2.

This is a fingertip application. Delicacy is indicated.

3.

Apply finger to the nose bridge. Brush rhythmically and slowly in furwise direction.

*La Petite is best applied by a practitioner with an intimate knowledge of the subject.

Purrometer reading: II

Rating on the Purr Register: 4

La Petite engenders a remarkable sense of abandon. Experts consider this
simple application to be the natural prerequisite for the stimulation of
the Tummy Points (see page 45).

H5 The Transwhisker Cross Step

▲▲▲▲▲▲▲

Technique

1.

The side of the head must be accessible. Ensure subject is relaxed.

2.

This is a side-of-finger application. Proceed with caution. It is a precarious procedure.*

3.

Place finger at edge of subject's moist health indicator. Keeping the rest of the hand quite still, move forefinger in a furwise direction. Note position of whiskers behind finger. (A left-hand application is depicted here.)

*This application is not for fainthearted practitioners, nor should it be applied to timorous subjects.

 **Response**

Purrometer reading: 0

Rating on the Purr Register: 5

This is the regrettable result of the misapplication of the Transwhisker
 Cross Step. (Though it is not to say that the subject did not derive
 considerable pleasure from the activity.)

Ear Points

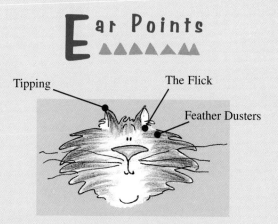

Tipping

The Flick

Feather Dusters

When the sun god Ra shines upon the ears of a
contented cat, all the world will be at leisure and
warm thoughts will abound.

E1 Feather Dusters

Technique

1.

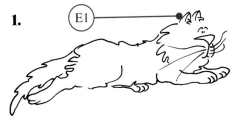

Subject's head should be alert and "in anticipation." The body may repose at leisure.

2.

Practitioner's fist in this instance is kept open and fluid, ready for a ripple application.*

3.

Nestle fist into area at the base of subject's ear. The second joint of fingers must make a continual rippling while the thumb remains taut and static.

*The success of Feather Dusters depends upon a confident delivery.

 # Response

Purrometer reading: V

Rating on the Purr Register: 5

The effect of the continual rippling is like that of a stone dropped into
   water. The subject vibrates from the ear outward. Certain subjects also
   dribble liberally from the mouth, adding to a general aquatic illusion.

E2 The Flick

▲▲▲▲▲▲▲

Technique

1.

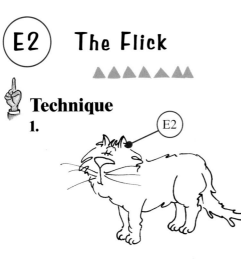

E2

Make contact immediately after subject has been indulging in a languid pastime, e.g., a yawn or a milk lap. Subject must be somnambulistic and cooperative.

2.

Practitioner's fingers need to work a sharp "reinvigorating" movement.* The middle finger is ideal for this purpose.

3.

Apply light staccato taps to lower back of ear. (Note cartilage.) Surprise, for the Flick, is not a disadvantage, unlike most other applications.

*The Flick is vital to the subject's realignment, grounding, and general orientation.

# Response

Purrometer reading: I

Rating on the Purr Register: 2

The subject will at first display an energized recovery, which will be
    followed by an antistatic maneuver (typically, a lightning-quick but
    substantial flick of the subject's ear).

E3 Tipping

Technique

1.

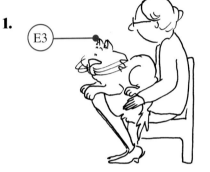

Have subject sit on practitioner's knee, facing outward.

2.

Practitioner will need to work with tips of thumb and forefinger to effect a pincerlike movement.

3.

Take tip of subject's ear between thumb and forefinger and rub rhythmically in a circular motion.

 # Response

Purrometer reading: V

Rating on the Purr Register: 5

Carried into a true ecstasy, the subject will rise to greet the application.
    (Practitioners are advised to wear protective clothing.)

Chin and Neck Points

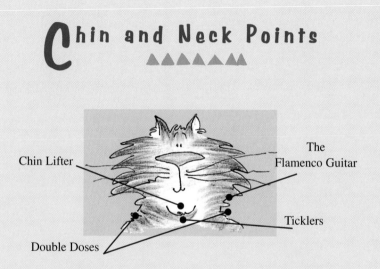

Chin Lifter

The
Flamenco Guitar

Ticklers

Double Doses

Behind the jaws of a pussycat rests the hope and
expectations of a lion.

Chin Lifter

▲▲▲▲▲▲

Technique

1.

Many positions are suitable for application of this Purr Point, provided chin is accessible.

2.

This is a continuous knuckle application. Practitioner's hands must move with the agility of a pianist warming up for an attack on the keys.

3.

Practitioner gently taps upper chin with forefinger. This activates subject's anticipation, and lower chin will be lifted. Practitioner then tickles under the chin using a continuous ripple effect.

 # Response

Purrometer reading: V

Rating on the Purr Register: 5

Somnolence gives way to decadence as the subject basks in the warm
   glow of the Chin Lifter. The practitioner will be invited to even greater
   excesses as the subject stretches and extends the chin to its uttermost.

Ticklers

Technique

1.  Subject should be in an erect pose.

2. Place forefinger in the "ready" position.

3.  Practitioner approaches subject from front; application should be administered in rapid furwise/ antifurwise movements.

 # Response

Purrometer reading: V

Rating on the Purr Register: 4

Ticklers is a glorious celebration of pleasure. The practitioner will be
tempted to repeat applications by such enticements as full-throated
purring, tail flicking, and furry vibrating on the part of the subject.

N1 The Flamenco Guitar

Technique

1.

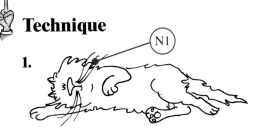

The subject should be lying in an uncurled position, on the side. The neck should be easily approachable.

2.

This is a one-handed application; the practitioner should have fingers taut and extended.

3.

Keeping the fingers rigid at all times, the practitioner strums the neck with the passion of a flamenco guitarist.

 # Response

Purrometer reading: II

Rating on the Purr Register: 4

Most subjects are disturbed from their torpor by the insistent Iberian
rhythm. Note the low purrometer reading—an indication of how
preoccupying the strumming can be.

N2 Double Doses

 Technique

1.

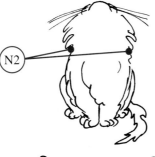

Ideally, apply this Purr Point immediately after application of Ticklers. Subject's neck will be perfectly positioned, and desire for further pleasuring will be at its height.

2.

Both hands must be made ready for a continuous knuckle application.

3.

Practitioner approaches subject from front. Hands must work simultaneously. Take care not to synchronize movements. The syncopation is what provides the thrill.

 **Response**

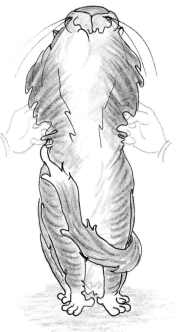

Purrometer reading: IV

Rating on the Purr Register: 5

The true origin of the expression "enwraptured" is illustrated in the
response to this application. Subjects will generally be transported into
some unrecognizable alter ego.

Tummy Points

The Plunge

The Full Fluff

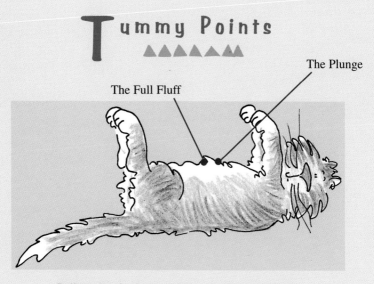

Believe that fur is not simply a convenient barrier worn to keep the cold at bay.

The Full Fluff

Technique

1.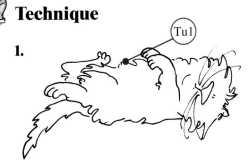

Subject should lie with tummy fully exposed in a location of extreme comfort.

2.

Practitioner's hand should be relaxed and feel very malleable.

3.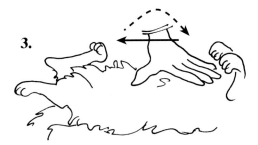

Gently lay hand upon subject's tummy. Stroke in single furwise motion, taking care to lift hand before renewing the stroke.

 **Response**

Purrometer reading: V

Rating on the Purr Register: 2

An application of the Full Fluff carries with it a considerable surprise for
the confident practitioner. Transported, as the applicant's hands are, on
a bedding of soft fluffy fur, the purring from the subject is soon trans-
ferred to the applicant until both are happily content.

(Tu2) The Plunge

▲▲▲▲▲▲▲▲

Technique

1.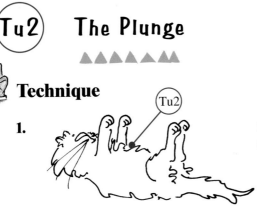

Ensure subject is in supine position.

2.

Hold hand thus as for a full-hand assault.

3.

Drop hand onto subject's tummy and move fingers rapidly at random.

 **Response**

Purrometer reading: IV

Rating on the Purr Register: 5

The Plunge is a highly dangerous application. However, it is also a Purr
   Point from which the subject will derive considerable pleasure.

Back and Tail Points

Spankers

Dancing the Limbo

The Bell Pull

Full pleasure does every cat explore with every back that's arched and every tail that's flicked.

B1   Dancing the Limbo

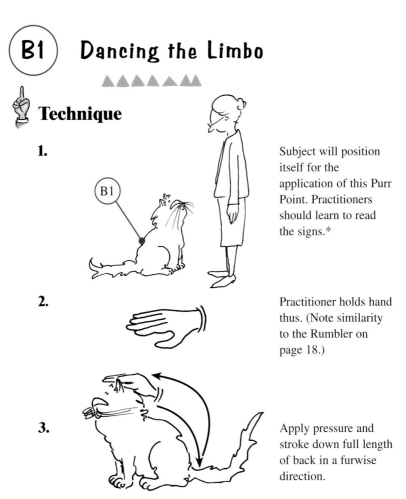

Technique

1.

Subject will position itself for the application of this Purr Point. Practitioners should learn to read the signs.*

2.

Practitioner holds hand thus. (Note similarity to the Rumbler on page 18.)

3.

Apply pressure and stroke down full length of back in a furwise direction.

*If the subject adopts this position and then commences to "weave," it is more likely to be in preparation for the Ultimate Pleasure (see page 63).

 # Response

Purrometer reading: II

Rating on the Purr Register: 3

The most intriguing aspect of this Purr Point is the fact that the subject
   behaves as if avoiding the very pleasure craved.

B2 Spankers

1. Spankers is one of the few Purr Points best approached with an element of surprise. Subject must be standing.

2. Hold hand out and keep rigid.

3. Make firm, rapid patting motions at the precise point of pleasure.

Response

Purrometer reading: 0

Rating on the Purr Register: 5

Despite the Purrometer reading, some experts even attribute the accolade
the "Ultimate Pleasure" to Spankers. (Suspect proclivities are also
referred to in Knuckle Dusters on page 20.)

Ta1 The Bell Pull

✍ **Technique**

1.

Position subject in indulgent position on practitioner's lap. Allow to relax totally.

2.

Practitioner's hand should be held in ready-to-grasp position.

3.

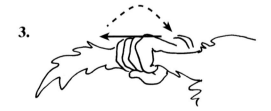

Unfold tail from "at ease" position and grasp in fist. Run hand furwise down tail. To repeat, release grasp slightly.

Response

Purrometer reading: IV

Rating on the Purr Register: 4

Carried into a frenzy of pleasure the subject will unleash a primordial
energy causing the practitioner to "stretch-the-lap." This additional
muscle manipulation provides exquisite secondary pleasure.

Leg Points

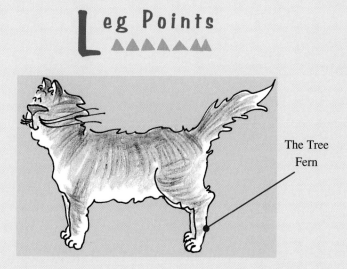

The Tree
Fern

If the legs are fleet and the paws are strong then the human will be in thrall to a panther.

(L1) The Tree Fern

▲▲▲▲▲▲▲▲

☝ Technique

1.

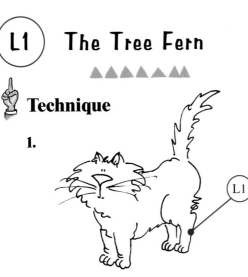

It's best if practitioner approaches a standing subject. The black stumps at back of leg must be accessible.

2.

Practitioner holds hand thus.

3.

Using inside of forefinger, practitioner strokes leg stumps downward. (Note: The fur at this site is generally erect and thus a furwise/antifurwise direction is difficult to identify.)

Response

Purrometer reading: II

Rating on the Purr Register: 3

The subject will willingly accept the opportunity to contort, achieving a
   coy appearance in the process. Practitioners may well find they contort
   in the same manner in order to assess the true level of pleasure being
   attained.

The Ultimate Pleasure

Only when caresses have touched the fur of the cat from one extremity to the other will the full picture of pleasure be truly revealed.

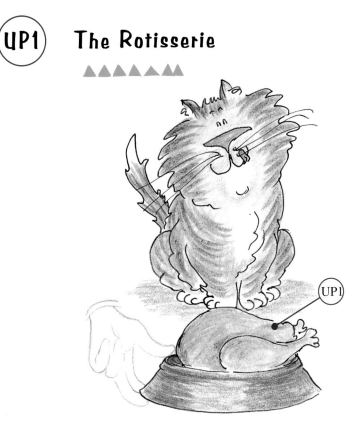

Purrometer reading: V

Rating on the Purr Register: 5

This Purr Point is named in honor of the circular motion that is taken by the subject's tongue when met with the prospect of this, the Ultimate Pleasure.